C000026345

NOT A CARE IN THE WORLD

RAVETTE PUBLISHING

© Bamforth and Company Limited 2013
Licensed by JELC Ltd
All rights reserved.

First published in 2013 by
Ravette Publishing Limited
PO Box 876, Horsham
West Sussex RH12 9GH

ISBN: 978-1-84161-373-4

THIS IS THE LIFE

LOTS OF REST

A TONIC NOW AND THEN

AND A LITTLE OF WHAT YOU FANCY DOES YOU GOOD

- FITZPATRICK -

YOU'RE NOT ASLEEP, MY LAD, NEITHER AM I!---THAT'S WHERE
YOU'RE HAVING YOUR HAT!

SHE'S GOT A FEW BARNACLES ON 'ER BOTTOM, BILL!

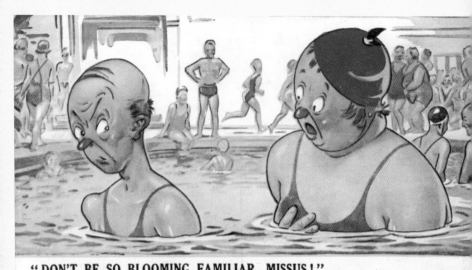

"DON'T BE SO BLOOMING FAMILIAR, MISSUS!"
"SORRY, MISTER, BUT YOUR HEAD'S JUST LIKE MY HUSBAND'S BEHIND!"

THE WIND'S A BIT NIPPY THIS MORNING, DON'T YOU THINK

OH! BUT IT IS LUVVLY HERE. I AINT CLICKED YET, BUT I'M LIVING IN HOPES

MY WORD, IT DOESN'T HALF JOLT YOUR DINNER ABOUT ON THE DODGEM

MY WIFE USED TO HAVE AN HOUR GLASS FIGURE, BUT NOW MOST OF THE SAND HAS RUN TO THE **BOTTOM** !

PA GETS BLAMED FOR A LOT HE DOESN'T DO, OTHERWISE WE'RE HAVING A GOOD TIME HERE

"THERE'S SOMETHING ABOUT THIS PLACE THAT TICKLES MY FANCY!"

E' BUT IT IS COLD WHEN IT GETS UP TO HERE

CLICKED AT LAST!
I THOUGHT MY TURN WOULD COME SOONER OR LATER

GO ON, SMACK IT, DAD! I WON'T TELL MOTHER

THIS IS THE PLACE FOR PUTTING THE WIND UP YOU.
IT'S A GOOD JOB WE HAD A WASH DAY BEFORE WE CAME AWAY

"LETTING MYSELF GO—I'M AS DAFT AS THEY MAKE 'EM THIS WEEK, BUT WHO CARES. I'M ENJOYING MYSELF!"

ENJOYING MYSELF FINE—
I'M ON A NICELY BALANCED DIET!

HAVING A **SPORTING** HOLIDAY!

MORNINGS–
SPORT OF THE WORKING MAN

AFTERNOONS–
SPORT OF KINGS

NIGHTS–
SPORT OF SPORT

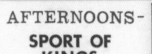

THERE ARE LOTS OF GAMES PLAYED ON THE BEACH HERE AND THEY'RE NOT ALL CRICKET!

"THERE'S NOTHING LIKE SEA AIR FOR FILLING YOUR LUNGS!"

ON THE BEACH AFTER DARK!
HURRY UP THE TIDES COMING IN!
I WISH YOU'D GET YOUR FINGER NAILS CUT!
BLIMEY THESE PEBBLES ARE HARD!
IF I SAID YOU HAD A NICE FIGURE— WOULD YOU HOLD IT AGAINST ME?
HELP!
STOP IT— YOU'RE TICKLING
I'M A MODEL YOU KNOW!
THIS IS A FINE TIME TO TELL ME YOU'RE NOT A BIRD!
IF IT WASN'T YOUR HAND WHO'S WAS IT?
GET STUFFED!
ITZPATRICK

Other titles available in this series ...

	ISBN	Price
Love Will Find a Way	978-1-84161-367-3	£5.99
Down with Drink	978-1-84161-368-0	£5.99
That's The Way To Do It!	978-1-84161-372-7	£5.99

HOW TO ORDER:

Please send a cheque/postal order in £ sterling, made payable to 'Ravette Publishing'
for the cover price of the book/s and allow the following for post & packing ...

UK & BFPO	70p for the first book & 40p per book thereafter
Europe & Eire	£1.30 for the first book & 70p per book thereafter
Rest of the world	£2.20 for the first book & £1.10 per book thereafter

RAVETTE PUBLISHING LTD
PO Box 876, Horsham, West Sussex   RH12 9GH
Tel: 01403 711443 Fax: 01403 711554 Email: ingrid@ravettepub.co.uk

Prices and availability are subject to change without prior notice